ORIGINALITY AND OTHER ESSAYS

ORIGINALITY

AND OTHER ESSAYS

BY

WILLIAM H. McMASTERS

Essay Index Reprint Series

BOOKS FOR LIBRARIES PRESS, INC.
FREEPORT, NEW YORK

First Published 1921
Reprinted 1967

LIBRARY OF CONGRESS CATALOG NUMBER:
67-28759

PRINTED IN THE UNITED STATES OF AMERICA

TO MY WIFE

A PHANTASY

Came a sunbeam to my window,
  Where a shadow was at play;
Came a bright and happy sunbeam,
  And the shadow flew away.

Came a maiden to the threshold
  Of my aching heart, one day;
Came a fair and winsome maiden,
  And the heart-ache stole away.

PREFACE

One reason why this little volume of essays is turned loose on a defenceless world is because the supply of white paper is not yet exhausted. Also, the author's patience in trying to get them printed in regular publications is quite exhausted.

The third, and best reason, for its appearance is that American publishers are of the unanimous opinion that there isn't any public demand whatsoever for a volume of essays from anybody on any subject. Under the circumstances what else is there for me to do, but offer them and hope for the worst?

THE AUTHOR

CONTENTS

ON ORIGINALITY

ON ORIGINALITY

THE word "Originality" is so often misused that I think it only fair to start with a clear presentation of my idea of the word.

Originality, as I understand it, is the capacity of doing something worth while and first. A man who can establish a school of painting as different from all other painting as were Corot's paintings from those of his time, is an originator. A man who can think along lines as trail-blazing as did Carlyle, is an original thinker—possesses originality. I am sorry for that kind of a man. His very capacity will make him lonesome.

If you were to walk on your hands, with your feet in the air some afternoon from Thirty-fourth Street to Forty-second, along Fifth Avenue, you would not be doing an original thing. You might think it original because you were the first to do it. But you have my assurance that it has been considered hundreds of times by many people, some of whom were temporarily sober, and been abandoned because they didn't consider it worth while.

To do merely the unusual, the bizarre, the different, the first-time thing, is not to accomplish the original. If it isn't worth something to yourself and to others it is not original in the true sense. So far as I see there isn't anything worthy of the modification of a clean-cut adjective that doesn't measure up to a certain standard.

In my youth I was told that there was always a demand for originality. The man who could think clearly along new lines, the man with real ideas, the man who could devise striking improvements, write new plays, new stories, (I am not so sure but that new essays were included) could command his own terms. The man who could do any or all these things was to have honors heaped upon him. I believed it. What young man, in or out of school, hasn't swallowed the bait that he sees floating in the silent pool of his young dreams, only to find out that he has been hooked, landed and sold in the fish-market of experience?

I know that I was first hooked with a worm bait and floundered in the grass so hard that I found my way back into the cool waters—more wary for my bleeding gills. The next time I was caught with a fly, but I escaped again by flopping out of the boat. Sport finally gave me up as a bad job and commercialism landed me in a net— a painless proceeding, it is true, but with no chance for escape. Into the basket and on with the course that follows the soup.

Into the net they go, mackerel, shad, salmon, black-bass, pickerel, perch, sharks, flounders, blue fish, tarpon, horn-pouts, jelly-fish, whales, sun-fish, star-fish, minnows and piscatorial youth that Ike Walton never knew or heard of—their visions blighted, their hopes blasted, their ideas ravished, their originality gone forever, to supply the greedy table of commercialism.

Once in the modern field of commercialism, the man with an original idea in his head is notified by some telepathic message that any change from the regular routine means cutting off his income. He becomes an automatic attachment to the hum-drum, a sort of a hum-drum-stick as it were. A wife and a family insure his helplessness for his life-time, unless—

Unless! Oh, that saving clause in every writ-ten statement. How restful to retrace one's steps and kick over every hurdle taken on the way out. In the case of originality, the ability to differ and differ intelligently, with reasons for the dif-ference, the word "unless" marks the bumper at the end of the side track. We will now go back onto the main line.

All those things I stated about originality being smothered with the de-oxygenized air of com-mercialism are true, unless—

Unless the fire of originality is the undying flame of genius, unless it is the ceaseless light that nature gives to some of her favored sons and daughters and tells them to go forth into the dark places.

When that light is once turned on in a human brain, all the avarice of business, all the commercialized powers of the world, all the grinding routine that deadens the faculties of ordinary people, merely makes the light of originality to shine the brighter, for darkness is the greatest background one can have against which to display light.

Originality is intelligent independence. Like all independence it must be fought for and paid for. Why should the possessor of originality complain? Hasn't he something that few possess? Isn't it worth more to him than all the country houses, the yachts, the limousines and the bank balances of all the men he knows? If the man with originality doesn't think it worth more than mere wealth, if he complain because it isn't readily saleable like the capacity to lay bricks or chauffeur a motor car, then he is not worthy, and the unworthy do not long retain possession of originality.

What if there is only a restricted market for originality! What if most editors are afraid of it, most play producers shy at it, and most publishers throw up their hands or run at the sight of it? It can't be helped. These are the commercialized handlers of routine things.

But somewhere, somehow, sometime there will be an editor, a producer, a publisher who understands. He is a kindred spirit. He is waiting for the one who is original; he has waited long. For his sake, and the sake of all those who will appreciate it Originality should keep up the fight till it wins.

To do something worth while and first!

Isn't it worth all the sacrifices, all the rebuffs, all the heartaches, all the lonesome vigils, the disappointments that it costs?

Maybe Lincoln could tell us. Maybe Grant knows. I am sure that Milton would be glad to set our minds at rest on the question if the wires from Mount Olympus were working.

Perhaps each of us can answer it in a way most satisfactory to himself. I am sure that I have the right answer in my own mind if only I cared to disclose it.

ON THE IMPENETRABILITY OF IGNORANCE

ON THE IMPENETRABILITY OF IGNORANCE

WHEN an intelligent man enters into a discussion with a man of total ignorance, he is at a disadvantage because he has to do the thinking for both sides. He is at another disadvantage because he has to express his thoughts in language that the ignorant man will understand. He is at another disadvantage because he has to treat the ignorant man as an equal and in order to do that he has consciously to lower himself. He can't lift the ignorant man up and in order to be equals in the discussion the intelligent man must put himself on a plane beneath him.

Thus we find a man, out of his regular environment, fighting with arms that he cannot use to advantage and being forced at all times to furnish arms and ammunition for his adversary. Is it worth the effort?

To this question, I say "No!" emphatically. I have never seen a discussion between ignorance and intelligence where ignorance didn't come off victorious. It can't be otherwise. The methods are so different, the disadvantages under which the intelligent man must labor, are so overwhelming, that no good can possibly come of the contest.

19

The reason why intelligence cannot compete with ignorance in a friendly discussion can be arrived at by analysis. We all know the capacity, the straightforwardness and the general mental-honesty of an intelligent man. He is intelligent because he thinks. He goes through a mental process, correlates ideas, adds, subtracts and divides thoughts, striving to arrive at a sane and therefore an intelligent conclusion.

On the other hand, the ignorant man doesn't think, because he has never been trained to think. His mentality can't get any further than a baby with its blocks, trying to build a house. His ignorance is impenetrable, in-so-far as immediate mental activity is possible.

In addition to his density he usually has several traits that assist materially in making it impossible to state even your own views without starting a wrangle and a wrangle is not a discussion.

The man of ignorance is always positive that he is right, regardless of the subject. He is a mental cheat and therefore suspicious of everybody. He can comprehend people as being only of the same frame of mind as himself. If he knew enough to appreciate an honest difference of opinion he wouldn't be ignorant. He is always proud of his ability to interrupt and figures that every interruption counts a point as though he were playing a game of mental slap-jack. Lastly, he knows that he can always say "I don't believe it" at the end of a discussion and from his long experience with other men "who tried to argue with him," he is quite sure that he can exasperate you and make you show your temper before the discussion is finished.

I feel that ignorant people should be treated kindly, be allowed to come into the front room if their hands and face have been washed, be allowed to tell everybody how much money they have made in selling clothes, or automobiles, in the stock-market, or wherever their ignorance commands the highest market price, but they should not be allowed to enter into discussions in which intelligent analysis may help to illuminate a truth or widen the scope of some public question.

Feed ignorance with predigested mental food only, otherwise you will have a case of ignorantia dyspepsia on your hands and for that there is no medicinal cure.   An operation on the dome is the only hope for the patient.   So be on your guard.

ON STICKING TO THE SUBJECT

ON STICKING TO THE SUBJECT

IF the object of a discussion is to arrive at an intelligent conclusion, I maintain that it is necessary to stick to the subject, else the time involved is wasted.

Nobody will disagree from this abstract proposition and yet I find it extremely difficult to get people to stick to the subject matter. Evidently the desire to wander far afield is so common as to present a good subject for comment and analysis.

Let us take, for example, any question of public interest and see how two average Commuters would discuss it while making the trip from their home station to the city, any morning.

"I see that Harding declares for more preparedness," says Commuter No. 1, by way of opening.

"So I see," replies Commuter No. 2, "and a fine mess we would be in if we followed his views. We would have another war on our hands in less than six months if we went in for all this preparation at this time."

"Why!" answers No. 1, raising his eyebrows, "I am surprised that anybody can disagree with the President on such a self-evident National need."

25

"Bryan doesn't agree with him, does he?" asks No. 2.

"Bryan has never been right on anything," answers No. 1. "Look at 16 to 1. Where would we be today if we had 16 to 1?"

"It wasn't Bryan's fault that 16 to 1 failed, was it? Didn't Alaska gold and South African gold come in to relieve the stringency?" retorts No. 2.

"What if it did?" asks No. 1, "Wouldn't these discoveries have been made, anyhow? Somebody is always discovering something. Everybody isn't a Doctor Cook."

"No! but Dr. Cook cleaned up his little pile on a lecture tour and that was what he was after. Get the public's money is the rule, nowadays. Look at this Dempsey, the new World's Champion. He won't fight. All he does is pose in the movies for the money," avers No. 2.

"Some people try to deliver the goods. They are not all fakers. There's Speaker of the Indians. He gives the public the best he's got. And it pays, doesn't it?" suggests No. 1.

"Well! he got all the breaks, didn't he? If the Red Sox were in shape he wouldn't have got any better than runner up," replies No. 2.

"I don't know about that," answers No. 1. "I always figured that batters are needed to win games and the Indians surely had a fine bunch of swatters."

"Swatters are all right, in their way," suggests No. 2, in a heavy voice, "but finesse counts in the end.   Otherwise, how is it that Senator Lodge was right on the League of Nations?"

"He never was right in his life," shouts No. 1. "Why! look at . . . "

The train having now arrived at the terminal and there being no further need of continuing the discussion, the two debators roll up their morning papers and walk down the aisle of their car, each satisfied that he has vanquished the other in a clear discussion of the question of "preparedness."

This may appear to many to be an exaggerated example of a discussion among men who meet in everyday intercourse.   To others I am afraid that it will appeal as a logical discussion, and that an intelligent conclusion was reached.   Such is the hold that mind-wandering has got upon us all that I needs must have a care or in an analysis of this vagary I inadvertently creep into the very error that I am hopeful to correct.

Therefore I say, without further parley, that in an essay on Sticking to the Subject the safest thing to do, in order to avoid getting away from the subject, is to end the essay before the text is forgotten by the reader.   Hence, the end.

ON THE GENTLE ART OF PADDING

ON THE GENTLE ART OF PADDING

I DO not desire to take away from Business Engineers, graft investigators, or Efficiency Experts any of their professional duties in connection with padded pay rolls, padded voting lists or padded Government war contracts. But there are other spots than these where padding is practised to such an extent that it is wasting the time of the public in a manner almost unbelievable.

I refer to padded novels, padded plays, padded speeches, padded sermons, padded moving picture shows, padded conversations, padded editorials, padded short stories, padded interviews, padded advertisements, padded legislative reports, hearings, committee meetings and so on, all padded until the meat is lost and only the shell of the nut is ever seen.

I shall not give examples of padding in all these lines of more or less intense thought. Padded commentaries are even worse than other forms of expression. A few examples will suffice. The others can readily be discerned, after the few are stripped of their superfluity.

As to novels, I firmly believe that ninety-five novels out of every one hundred that pour from the publishing house binderies in ever-increasing streams could be cut down from fifty per-cent to ninety per-cent and be greatly improved in the reduction. The shorter the story, the clearer must the plot stand out and a story without a well defined plot is a pretty poor story. I recall a Society Novel (publishers' classification) that I tried to read, quite recently. Its author was strong on the ways in which he could make his characters talk. On three consecutive pages, two of his characters were engaged in talking.

During this three minute conversation they spoke "fiercely," "surprisedly," "suggestively," "flippantly," "laughingly," "incredulously," "banteringly," "querulously," "inadequately," "slowly," "reservedly," "vehemently," "longingly," "tremulously," "almost venomously," "impetuously," "with lowered eyes," "blushingly," "with head erect," "as though loath to change the subject," "with disdain," "with hauteur," "with deep feeling," "coldly," but when I read " 'Then you can't go?,' asked Herbert, inquiringly," I closed the book. Such stuff isn't writing. It is padding with defenceless words that are wonderful if used rightly.

Then the movies. I was compelled to take over an hour to see six long reels unwind themselves to tell a story that could have been told in ten minutes, without leaving out one essential that affected in any way the lives or fortunes of the hero and heroine. Fifty minutes of pure nonessentials in order to get over a fairly good 10-minute story.   Think of the time wasted by producer, audience and the general breaking down of brain power on people who, after a while, become so used to this sort of entertainment that a keen, well-conceived plot, filmed at tension speed, can't be followed by their slow-moving brains.   It will not be long before the efforts of an intelligent author and a conscientious producer are wasted in trying to give the public something worth-while.

How many times have you gone to hear a speaker on a subject in which you were interested and been forced to listen to a dozen of "that reminds me" brand of anecdotes, seven interruptions prefaced with " and I might recall in this connection," four "while it is not directly connected with our topic, nevertheless, etc.," and at the end of the speech gone home thoroughly convinced that you had wasted your time?

Is there any need of taking up the other instances of padding?   Not unless I wish to do a little padding on my own account.   So I will let you think over the others in your own way.   To padders, I suggest cutting out the padding.   You will never know the joy of delivering the goods until you do.   Headliners don't do it.   Nobody pads who isn't ashamed of his true shape.   And the truth shall make you free,—from padding.

ON THE MATTER OF ADVICE

ON THE MATTER OF ADVICE

ADVICE is a peculiar commodity. Those who have the capacity to give good advice generally have too much sense to waste their time trying to get rid of it.

I am not referring to "advice of counsel." That is a different kind of advice altogether. It has the redeeming feature of being paid for and when a man pays for something he generally uses it in order to get value for his money.

Are you one of those innocent souls who are always giving good advice? If so, I hope you cease your activity.

As I recall the last member of your fraternity whom I met, he was deeply grieved over several business men who had "all gone wrong because they didn't take my advice," as he put it. I have yet to hear him tell me of a solitary instance where a man had taken his advice and achieved something because of it.

Giving free advice is a sad waste of effort. In the first place, no man will act upon it unless he is already inclined to do so. Secondly, when a man lays his case before you, the idea that he is asking your advice is a polite fabrication. He merely is suggesting that he is doing so, while as a fact his real object is to acquaint you with his personal activity.   He wants to talk to somebody, being a natural gossip or gadder, and he plays upon your propensity for "giving advice" in order to get an audience.

Just the way a doting father of a three-year-old infant prodigy will wait patiently for hours while another doting father of a four-year-old genius tells "what a vocabulary Emil has developed," simply because he wishes to spread upon the records a conversation that he had that morning with Jonas in which Jonas actually pointed out of the window and said "Oh! Papa, it's going to rain," and only three years old, eight months ago.

The times when you can actually give a man some real advice and be sure of his taking it and acting upon it are very few.

My mind now recalls vividly the numerous precious hours I have wasted in listening to hard-luck stories, and advising the tellers of the stories and also of the many times when I have made suggestions to men in their business or vocations out of mere friendliness.   In the matter of the hard-luck stories I am unable to instance one case wherein the advisee has paid any attention to my opinion.   In the matter of the business men or the professional men on whom I have showered my views, I am able to cite many cases where the advice has been taken, but never once where

I received so much as a "thank you" for having made the suggestion.

I presume most men like to pose as the originators of every idea upon which they act and which reaches a successful end. They give credit only to somebody else when failure attends the venture. Most men can make a better excuse than they can an execution.

So I came to the conclusion, that if my advice wouldn't be taken by those who needed it most and was stolen by those who could well afford to pay for it, that I would hereafter give advice only to myself and always sell it to others.

That is why, in this brief discussion of the question, I have sold you whatever advice you may be able to glean from it, knowing full well that you wouldn't take it if you got it for nothing.

ON THE CONTRACTING OF HABITS

ON THE CONTRACTING OF HABITS

WE are being constantly warned against bad habits,—told how easy it is to acquire them, how hard it is to break them, but, all summed up, this advice doesn't seem to be the right sort. We all know our bad habits, acknowledge them to ourselves, at least, and would gladly rid ourselves of them. But we don't do so and there is a good reason. Trying not to do something is so lacking in initiative, so nugatory a thing that most of us dismiss the idea almost without a second thought.

Why not take up with the Conservation plan? Why not turn our habit-making tendencies into assets? It can be done, readily enough, and just so soon as we have acquired enough good habits to occupy our attention, the detrimental ones will have disappeared. Of all kinds of habits,—good or bad—I am sure there is a limit to the number that any one person can keep.

I have never smoked at all, so I do not feel free to discuss the habit of smoking, except as a general observer of it. It always seemed to me that an after-dinner cigar or cigarette was a mere waste of time. At least, one might pick up the habit of reading some of the best philosophy, while puffing away at the weed. Any man who will put his mind on Epictetus and try to smoke at the same time should be so well occupied mentally that his physical demands will become less and less. It is worth the experiment.

One who has acquired the habit of demanding an appetizer in order to enjoy his dinner and the habit of eating pepsin tablets to settle his dinner after the appetizer has forced him to eat a big one, can well afford to drop the appetizer at one meal and chew every morsel of food very thoroughly before swallowing it. When he finds that his taste is awakened, that he doesn't need to eat so much, that hitherto despised foods take on a pleasantness that was formerly reserved for highly spiced foods, that he doesn't need his pepsin tablet and that he eagerly awaits his next meal in order to test the experiment once more, then that person has made one good habit grow where two bad ones grew before. I know, because I have experienced it.

These are purely physical habits. When it comes to rearranging the habits of the mind, just think of the countless opportunities before you.

Instead of jotting down everything in a little memorandum book, as though you were a walking card-index system, try to remember an appointment, a name, a date, an amount or a purchase to be made. The very effort of trying to remember it, even if you forget it and can't recollect just what it was, will so stimulate your mind along that particular channel that the next time you make a mental note it will register and stay registered. Try it for yourself. Don't merely tell somebody else about it.

The habit of forgetting names, forgetting faces, forgetting anything is sheer carelessness. Make every impression register. You often hear people say "I can't remember names," or "I can't remember faces." You would almost think they were boasting of an accomplishment. They are so reconciled to this bad habit of their mind that they take it as a sign of genius. It is merely a habit and can be corrected by substituting a positive brain action in place of a brain inactivity.

Begin to say "I never forget a face," or "Remembering names is my hobby." Repeat every man's name in full, when you meet him and recall when you saw him last, even if it was only the day before. You will be surprised how your brain responds to this acceleration. It will become a fixed habit of the mind to remember. Once fixed, it need never be lost.

Why go through the list? Start with a simple foible! Substitute its opposite! Make a beginning! Furnish your own incentive for the first one! No man thinks unless he thinks for himself. It isn't real thinking, otherwise. All thinking is habit. Thinking right is a good habit. It will never be acquired unless you start. Now is the only time.

ON NEW YORK—A CITY IN PROCESS

ON NEW YORK—A CITY IN PROCESS

I AM generally so worked up after a trip to New York that it takes days for me to return to the normal. Before my return to that state, I feel that a transcript of my impressions, set down in their vividness, may serve a useful purpose.

It has been the general idea of Americans and the American press to comment ad nauseam upon our biggest city. This has grown even more noticeable, recently.

Naturally, one carries to New York a craving to see some of the many things that our world-metropolis is supposed to possess. One sees the things, true enough. But of the environment, almost nothing has been said. Honesty would compel anybody, not self-hypnotized, to affirm a disappointment with which that of a blind man, accidentally taken into a movie show by his attendant, will not compare. His is merely negative disappointment. New York furnishes a positive one. We are compelled to see the show.

New York is a six-reel movie, with the film running backwards, sideways, cross-ways, but never in sequence. Nobody seems to be going anywhere, but is in an awful hurry to get there.

The idle rich work harder than the idol worshipping poor.

Nothing is finished in New York. Everything is being done over. It is a city in transit—rapid, near-rapid and over crowded.

The buildings are either too big or so small that they would be a joke in any country town's business center. Within two blocks of the new Pennsylvania station there are a dozen buildings so dilapidated and mean-looking that they could remain standing in Boston only if the Historical Society placed bronze tablets upon them and had them put on the itinerary of the seeing Colonial Boston autos.

The streets are the worst in the world—in or out of the war zone. Between 42nd street and the Woolworth Building, on Broadway, there isn't one block out of the sixty where the sidewalk is clear. Pavements are like rugs, in New York. They have to be taken up every few days and sent to the cleaner.

Dirt, bricks, lumber, stone-piles, contractors' offices, repair gangs, bags of cement, mortar beds, unwashed windows, signs without ceasing, a feverish jumble—that is the Great White Way, to which George Cohan's regards must be given.

And the people who inhabit this city, or infest it rather, because it can't be a habitation, what of them? Do they redeem it? No! dear readers,

they do not.   They are so busy trying to redeem
the mortgages that the landlords of New York
have placed upon their souls that they have no
personalty or personality left to redeem the city.
It is beyond redemption, so far as they are concerned.

In vain does the stranger look for the New
Yorker type, the man of the classy magazines.
Instead he sees nervous, gaunt-faced men by day,
and evening-clothed, dull-eyed, prematurely old
men at night, hurrying, hustling, scrambling,
rushing, whither nobody knows.

Search and you search in vain for the society
woman, the queens of beauty and culture that the
Sunday papers chronicle and our society authors
depict so minutely.

They are not.   In their stead you will see
shrimps of women, with their wizened little faces
painted and powdered, you will see in the noonday
glare, fat, vulgar women, over laden with wraps
that give them an appearance of casks moving
in a pattering way along the board pavements.
New York is one endless plank sidewalk.

And the bright-faced boys of the old Alger
books.   Where are they?   Gone, with the New
York of pre-library, pre-Equitable Building, pre-
Bus, pre-tunnel days.   Their places are taken by
boys who cry the names of the evening and morning newspapers in foreign tongues.   There must

be some ordinance against an American-born boy selling newspapers in New York City.

The city has gone mad over merchandise, nothing else counts. It is the only thing that can interest a regular New Yorker. Everything in New York is for sale, including the honor of the City itself. To deny it would be considered dishonorable on the part of a New Yorker of the present day. Culture has been swallowed up by barter.

If a bell boy at any of the best known New York hotels were to page Ralph Waldo Emerson in a loud voice in the breakfast room, the only comment that it would create would be the remark from one end of the room to the other "I wonder what firm Emerson's buying for?"

New York is unfinished. But business goes on just the same. Business is continuous. Everything else in New York is subservient to business. If New York would only stop talking about its side shows, its buildings, its Broadway, its class, its style, its civic pride, and put a sign at every approach:

> BUSINESS GOING ON
> DURING ALTERATIONS

people would know what to expect and many outside visitors would be saved disappointment.
They would figure that one must put up with
much inconvenience during needed changes—and
New York surely needs a great many changes—
some of which have not yet been proposed by the
City fathers.

ON WHY NOT YESTERDAY?

ON WHY NOT YESTERDAY?

FOR two weeks I have been putting off something of importance that should be done. This is not the exception that proves the rule. It is the rule itself, and I am determined that this rule must be changed.

Why didn't I set myself to the task yesterday and do it? It isn't a hard thing to do, once I start it. It is only the starting that troubles and this has been a trouble of mine for so many years that I am trying to analyze my own failure in the hope that a correct analysis may help somebody else who is troubled in like manner.

What I should have done yesterday was easily the most important thing that confronted me and it is just as important today. Therefore, I cannot offer the excuse that something more important intervened. Such an excuse would be unworthy of my desire to be honest with myself.

The task was not one that should have been set off for a more opportune time. Yesterday was the ideal time. But I did something else. The fact that I can't find nearly as much fault with myself today for my neglect of yesterday as I would have found with myself a few years ago for a similar neglect is the reason why I am analyzing my condition. I am in danger. I must settle, once and for all, upon the reason and make it impossible for similar neglects to occur in the future.

It was not a matter of routine that was neglected. I am a slave to doing the routine thing at the routine time in the routine way. Except as a routine thing is a part of a great routine plan and that the whole plan is affected by a break in the chain, I have wholesome contempt for routine.

It was an unusual thing, something bigger than a routine thing, that I neglected to do—neglected to start. I put off starting it because I have allowed myself to contract the habit of deferring mental effort until an artificial stimulus starts something. I have not forced my habits to keep pace with my thoughts. My will power has habituated itself to trailing behind my imagination.

Will somnolence—a lethargy of concentration —a reticence to keep pace that I set for myself a few years ago, has laid hold upon me.

I realized suddenly that if I allowed it to overpower me I would become one of the self-satisfied hack writers that I have despised secretly as lacking initiative. Therefore, if I do not wish to become a hackenyed writer I must fight it and fight it openly. I must show that I am not afraid of it. Others have conquered it. I shall conquer it by recognizing it as an enemy, putting it on the defensive and starting at once and continuing until I have finished the task that I have neglected for two weeks.

Some may wonder what this task may have been that has so roused me to lay my mentality bare before a critical world. Let us have no secrets from each other. The confession of an English opium eater must not be the only open-minded confession in our language. Let this confession of mine be placed upon the records in all its nudity.

The task I had set for myself was to write a brief essay on mental laziness, known to students as procrastination and as the task is now finished I take my leave of it, with a profound feeling of relief. I can now return to routine work with a mind at peace with the world.

ON THE COMPETENT

ON THE COMPETENT

THE competent must fight without help. No aid societies collect for them—no relief Committees take cognizance of their needs.

They can be discouraged, they can be in debt, they can be ready to give up the struggle, but no life-preserver is thrown to them. They must either sink or swim on their own resources. It is one of the essentials of competency that it must take care of itself.

Stupidity, degeneracy, incapacity, viciousness, all receive their quota of help from every source. The drunken reporter is excused for falling down in his assignments—the dope-fiends are cared for by the authorities—the stupid men in public life are aided by everyone and in many instances have been known to run along for years, hiding their stupidity, covering up their utter lack of initiative.

But those who can—the competent, the thinkers, the men or the women with vision, talent or capacity—must fight for every inch of ground, must pay in their heart's blood for every ounce of success.

And the reason? Why! there isn't any reason for it. It simply is so. Watch a crowd of men rush to lift up a fallen drunkard from the side-walk, see the subscriptions that pour into every request for aid for people unknown to the donors, and then check up the men who have been com-pelled to fight discouragement, ill-luck and pov-erty even with the talent and the genius of a Mozart, a Michael Angelo or a Tolstoi at their command.

Competency may be overlooked but it never is a beggar. It is too proud. It is a thing in itself —always was and always will be. It stands or falls—a complete structure, leaning on nothing, asking nothing but the right to do.

Competency is. We can say no more.

ON CHAMBERS OF COMMERCE

ON CHAMBERS OF COMMERCE

A CHAMBER OF COMMERCE is one of the growths of American life that is peculiar in many respects. So far as I am aware, no Chamber of Commerce ever had anything to do with Commerce. To a great extent a Chamber of Commerce is as free from Commerce as a Board of Trade is from Trade.

I presume that the first Chamber of Commerce was organized as a joke. Some jocose one said to a few kindred spirits, "Whillikins isn't any too busy, lately. Why not start a Chamber of Commerce and make him President?"

Like many another careless remark, turned loose to wander forever in the realms of telepathy, this one started on its way.

"Why not!" says the second Village Jokester, so The Bollweville Chamber of Commerce was organized. Whillikins falls in with the idea as it gives him a title and Mrs. Whillikins jumps at it because it smacks of social advancement. When the organizers find that Whillikins intends to have handsome embossed stationery and an office over the hardware emporium, they decide that it might be a good plan to have a full list of officers. Not caring to breed jealousy among the organizers, they decide to give them all the same title, so there come into being about thirty Honorary Vice-Presidents, which exhausts the list of all the organizers. That accounts for the big lists of Honorary Vice-Presidents in all Chambers of Commerce.

It was observed, shortly after the organization of the Bollweville C. of C. that nobody cared to join unles he was given a title, so a Board of Directors came to pass. As the joke, or rather as the Chamber began to grow, it was necessary, in order to keep down the engraving bills, to put all new members on Committees, with permission to tell their friends who were not members. Meantime a Secretary and an Assistant Secretary had duly become planted in permanent quarters in an inside office, these being the paid or reason-why officials of the Chamber.

Years after the first Chamber of Commerce was organized and most of the Charter members had either died natural deaths or laughed themselves into premature graves at the joke they had perpertrated on the town, strange business men began to come and do business. Not that the Chamber of Commerce had sent for them. Certainly not. It is one of the fundamental rules of every well conducted Chamber of Commerce that they will never send for anybody or anything.

Dignity is the basic principle of all C's of C.   So the strangers, being a jolly lot, mistook the Chamber of Commerce for a bunch of highbrows or austere standoffs, and organized a Business Men's Association.

Everybody was eligible, from the owner of the Hardware Store up to the owner of the White House Lunch, up indicating the hill at the other end of Main Street from the Hardware Store where the White House Lunch nightly was driven by Freeman Bently, Egg and Coffee Specialist. Naturally, the Business Men's Association soon began to assume proportions as you might say.

More as a narrative, rather than in the form of an essay, we must rapidly chronicle the big dinner of the Business Men's Association at the Bollweville House, the nomination, election to membership, issuing of certificates and mailing of same, all in one evening of John D. Rockefeller, Frank Vanderlip, J. Pierpont Morgan, Henry Ford, Warren G. Harding, William Jennings Bryan and the Governors of all the known states of the Union, with a story of same in the Gazette.   Follow the Executive Meeting of the Chamber of Commerce and the overtures to the officers of the Business Men's Association to consolidate, the real reason being jealousy but the reason given to the press being "Co-operation and the fact that the Chamber has outgrown its old quarters and is going to build a new building of its own, fitted in every way to its great work."

Nothing can stop a Chamber of Commerce that has consolidated a few times with other bodies of a like uselessness. It always builds a building and names it after itself. It has become a fixed institution. By holding adverse possession for more than 20 years, it has reached a legal position that is unimpeachable. All the hotairian rights now run with it. In fact it is just as safe and just as permanent a fixture in the public mind as the idea that a Public Service Commission has something to do with improving the services of Public Service Corporations.

Thus we are confronted with determining upon a general definition of a Chamber of Commerce for future reference. The following is submitted, subject of course to the approval of the "Committee of 125 on additions to or subtractions from the By-Laws," at the next subsequent meeting thereafter.

A Chamber of Commerce is an unwieldy body of men who are totally averse to any increase in Commerce, divided into political, social and religious cliques and whose main object in life appears to an outsider to consist of welcoming the incoming and speeding the parting President at a dinner that taxes the capacity alike of the diners and the main dining room of the leading Hotel.

One thing can be said for a Chamber of Commerce and nobody will deny it. The bigger it becomes, the better. The idea is this. A small Chamber of Commerce might work untold harm in a Community because it might be taken seriously. But a great, big overgrown Chamber of Commerce can't hurt anybody because "too many people are next," as the slang writers have it, meaning the enjoyment of close mental juxtaposition.

So, if you would save your city, join your Chamber of Commerce. The joke is on you, true enough, but what's the harm? The Secretary and his Assistant have to be paid in order to keep all the membership cards up to date so that visitors can be told that "The Bollweville Chamber of Commerce is now the largest in America east of the Connecticut River."

ON OVER-ENTHUSIASM

ON OVER-ENTHUSIASM

THE tendency to over-enthusiasm has so many forms that I will not attempt to touch except illustratively upon it. From a purely mental standpoint it generally consists of an indiscriminate use of adjectives, expletives and modifiers of various kinds.

I know certain men who go to the wildest extremes in their enthusiasm of the moment. If it is an editorial that has attracted their attention, it isn't a mere editorial when they hand it over for your educational benefit, it is "by all odds the finest editorial I have ever read" or the tender is prefaced with some such remark as "I want you to read this editorial. If you don't say it settles the question beyond the shadow of a doubt, I shall be everlastingly surprised."

With all this preliminary adulation you naturally expect to find an editorial bristling with points and reeking with research and profundity. But you are surprised to read an ordinary, wishy-washy statement with which you don't agree and as for the question being settled beyond the shadow of a doubt, while you are quite willing to agree that the editorial settles the question positively, it settles it contrary to the hopes and wishes of the editor.   In fact it settles in a sort of reverse English, as Willie Hoppe might say.

The next day you meet your over-enthusiastic friend and this time he is voluntary advance man for a new restaurant that he has discovered in the market district.   It is always in the market district or some out of the way spot.   You simply must go with him as his guest to this restaurant. "Talk about your roast beef!   Wow! Wow! wait till you get a slab of the beef they serve at this place.   No style, understand.   Plain, like the service at the front in the European War Zone, but clean.   Everything is put into the quality of the beef, etc. etc."

Naturally you yield and follow him.   Through a labyrinth of streets, alleys and short cuts. Past sidewalks piled high with fruits and vegetables.   Finally, up a long flight of stairs, each one with an overhang of corrugated metal on it that nearly trips you at every step, and then to the restaurant plus.

Exuding appologia at everything that seems to displease you, Mr. Enthusiasm leads you to a table and flourishes you into the seat.   "Roast beef for two," he says to the waitress, and then continues his apology monolog for the surroundings, but dilates upon the treat in viands that is soon to be yours.   Comes the beef.   (Please note the new style of expression, introduced to show that other authors have no copyright on this rhetorical bunk.) Descends the knife. Likewise the fork . . .

Well! you should have known better. After the editorial incident you should have been able to guess well ahead that adjectives do not create roasts of beef. This beef that you have tackled is surely meat for repentance. Not con beef, exactly, but scarcely a beef, as Bacon said, of some kinds of books, "to be chewed and digested."

Sorrowfully you are reminded of the story of a young actor who played a Western town. The show wasn't very well received. In talking with the hotel clerk after the performance the actor said, "They didn't warm up very much, tonight."

"Didn't?" answered the clerk. "Well! that is a common thing here, lately. Nine times out of ten the press agent is better than the show."

Over-enthusiasm is fatal to the delivery of the goods. Over-enthusiasm of one's own ability in salesmanship or any line of productivity is sure to be checked up.

It starts with a slight exaggeration. Later it becomes a habit. Finally it becomes a fixed rule of conduct and in the end it so dominates one's mode of life that he will spend more time in useless enthusiastic outbursts than he spends in those activities on which his livelihood depends. He consolidates his side show with his big show by moving the main tent into the place where the tatooed man and the armless wonder should be the main attractions.

Joking aside, this over-enthusiasm for every thing from a Symphony concert down to the third number of a new movie reel that exploits the utter stupidity of a band of murderers, is a blight upon our civilization. It must be stopped, at once, or language will not pass at its face value at the mint of intelligence.

"How can it be stopped?" you ask. Well! as a mere suggestion I offer this solution.

First, stop it yourself. Second, ask your friends to stop it. Third, I will stop it.

So far as I am concerned I end "over-enthusiasm," right here.

ON MEN OF MYSTERY

ON MEN OF MYSTERY

FOR fear that you may be misled by the title of this little etude, I assure you in the opening paragraph, that it is not my intent to lead you into the realms of the occult. But I would, with your kindly indulgence, unburden myself of a life-long contempt that I have held for certain people who shroud the commonplace with mystery and who draw a veil of utter secrecy over the beautiful face of lucidity.

In the vernacular of the burlesque houses I ask "where do they get this stuff?" It surely is a mystery to me, to most everybody else and I am not quite sure but to the mysterious ones, themselves.

While these Secret Service exemplars generally exercise their talents at all seasons of the year, it is in political contests that they show to the greatest advantage. Whether it is in the election of a Governor, a Mayor, an Alderman or in the settlement of a great question involving liberties of half the human race—woman suffrage—it matters not to the mysterious ones. They will avoid the direct, speak only in parables and implore you "not to breath a word of it," while keeping you thoroughly in the dark as to what it refers.

I know one of these mystery purveyors who is so saturated with "inside camouflage" that it effects his carriage. He sways his shoulders as he walks, with a sort of Hawaiian dance motion. This is accentuated by covert glances from side to side as a sort of optical accompaniment to his shoulder song. Tripping lightly along on the balls of his feet, he meets an acquaintance, or victim.

"Hello Ben!" says the victim, "how is Gloss coming out, next Tuesday?" Being interested in politics, he puts a direct question. But does he get a direct answer? He certainly does not. Ben is a "mysterious" person. He hasn't given a direct answer to anybody, anywhere, anytime to any question since he failed to pass the entrance exams to the village High School.

Acquaintance is waiting for an answer. Ben looks all around the vicinity. He evidently is afraid that he is being shadowed. He grips his victim by the lapels of his coat. He makes as though to speak, changes his mind, takes another survey of the location and drags his prey about ten feet to the left. Indoors or outdoors, the same formula is used. The victim never finds fault. Isn't he going to get the "straight dope" right from headquarters.

With his man safely planted, Ben takes yet one more flitting panoramic view of his new field of operations and whispers in a low tone, "What do you hear?"

Just imagine the disappointment anybody feels after all these maneouvers to receive a question when an answer was expected! But that is about all that these mystery mines yield. They assay about 60 per cent mystery and the rest pure fake. They yield nothing of a real marketable value at the smelter. They have never even been salted with good ore. They are absolutely valueless.

I have participated as publicity advisor in many campaigns, some of considerable importance. Every one of these campaigns had its army of mysterious ones always on the job. They filled the headquarters with an atmosphere of stealth. Their voices were always pitched in a stage whisper. It was "Sh! sh" here and "Sh! sh" there. They would pop their heads inside the door, take a mental inventory of the room, beckon to me with a backward jerk of the head to indicate that I must see them outside in the corridor.

Somehow I always hated to offend them and I invariably responded. The sum total of all I ever learned from the entire mystery squad could be contained in the following composite question, thrown at me in a throaty tremolo.

"Did you see the statement that so-and-so had in the Chronicle?"

Did I see it?   Naturally, having worked hours in writing it and having spent more hours with reporters and editors in order to have it appear. But why waste time?   I answer "yes", in order to get back to work, and Mr. Scotland Yard looks wise and puts two fingers of his left hand to his lips, as if to caution me against going too far.

"Nothing else you want to say to me?" he asks.

"No!" I reply.

"See you this afternoon then.   Don't let anybody know that we talked this over," and he disappears.

You might not believe that these are concrete examples of the way some men behave in politics. But the examples are just as concrete as the heads of the men involved.

Not one or two, but shoals of them, all mystery and no solution.   Over the phone, letters absolutely meaningless, childish references to the most obvious happenings as though dire happenings were to follow.

At first I was unable to understand it.   Later it began to dawn upon me.   Now I see the light. I shall never be fooled again.   These men of mystery are the men who elect candidates.   That is why they have to be mysterious.   No candidate can fight out in the open and win.   He must be obscured in the shadow of Teutonic Diplomacy or else he is destined to defeat. So the mysterious maurauder who couldn't deliver his own vote. He carries the mystery of the campaign into every successful candidate's office after his inauguration and mysteriously get a fat job and holds it in a most mysterious fashion.

If you don't believe me, ask any recent Governor or Mayor what was the reason for appointing any of the men whom he appointed. He will tell you "Sh! sh! I can't give you the real reason, but he did some great inside work for the party."

You think I am exaggerating the kind of men who are rewarded with political appointments. Ask any one of them, the next time you meet him what time it is? If he doesn't make you step ten paces to the left and whisper it into your ear, with a mysterious wink indicative of profound secrecy, then you may rest assured that he won't last out his term. His health is being undermined with the enormous work of his position. He isn't a regular. One season will see his finish.

And by the way, now that we have finished this matter, please don't tell anybody else about it! Let's keep it a secret. You know, "Sh! Sh!"

ON THE BUSY BUSINESS MAN

ON THE BUSY BUSINESS MAN

THE President of the largest bank in Boston is the most easily approached of any financial man in the city. The Presidents of numerous dinky little banks and trust companies can't be seen by anybody except after running the gauntlet of two or more secretaries. You can walk right into the office of the most influential man in New England, without the formality of sending in a card or even knocking at a closed door. The door of his office is open, the way is clear, you can see whether he is engaged with somebody else, when common politeness will hold you back. Otherwise you may enter and state your business.

The advertising manager of the largest circulated morning paper in America sits at a desk where anybody can speak to him, without leaving the public business office of the paper. But to see the advertising manager of the scrawniest sheet in Boston requires an official appointment, days in advance. I have often wondered if some of the enormous advertising business that appears in the big papers wasn't business that somebody had really intended placing in the scrawny little paper but had found it impossible to reach the advertising manager and give him the order.

The manager of the store that does the largest retail business of any store in Boston can be seen by anybody who thinks he has business with him, inside of half a minute after leaving the elevator at the office floor, unless he is occupied with somebody else. The fact that you are waiting generally speeds up the interview of the one ahead. The door is open so that the manager's time is not needlessly taken up. But at a little retail store across the street, which does less than one per cent of the big firm's volume of business, you will have to send in a history of your life by a fresh office boy, be interrogated by an equally fresh secretary and be compelled to wait in solitary confinement for hours before "Mr. Small will see you."

Having run into this peculiar phase of business life on many occasions, I began to give it more than a cursory thought. Why is it that the really big and successful men are so informal and the little inconsequential men so pompous? The big men never appear so busy that they can't attend to business. But the little men are invariably so "busy" that they make it impossible for one to explain his business in a business-like way and complete it.

After all, the answer is not complicated. It has nothing to do with the amount of business that any of these men are handling. It is purely a psychological problem and requires a psychological answer.

A big man in business is no different from a big man in any other walk of life. He is a big man and requires no outside evidences to prove it. He is sure of himself. He needs no secretary to tell you he is busy. His position, his own assurance of his bigness tells it to you. He knows you or anybody else will not try to occupy his time, needlessly. But a man of small calibre in business is no different from a small calibre man in any other activity. He is anxious to impress upon the world a capacity that he doesn't possess. So he starts with his secretary. He is afraid to appear not busy to his secretary. That would be fatal. So he is always looking over invoices, bills of lading, market reports or "talking with heads of departments." This latter is generally his last resort. He wants the secretary to tell the business world that "Mr. Small is the busiest man in town."

So you suffer, and wait, and look at your watch, and read your newspaper and count the letters on the door and make up all the words you can spell from PRIVATE OFFICE, and think what you are going to order for lunch, and go to sleep, and look at your watch again and finally see "Mr. Small" and learn only too late that all your time has been wasted. He isn't making any change until the middle of next year as "his policy has been thoroughly outlined and he never changes his policy" and "if you will see him in six months he will be glad to talk it over with you."

And the funny part of it is that you, your very self, are surprised when you read in the newspaper among "Business troubles" that "The Small Company has gone into the hands of a receiver," a few weeks after the visit when you were told that "our policy is outlined for the next six months."

ON DISTRIBUTION

ON DISTRIBUTION

DON'T be alarmed. I am not going to read you a lecture on the Distribution of Wealth or even on the Distribution of Intelligence. They will always be distributed unevenly. But the distribution of merchandise is a question that needs an answer if any economic question does.

I am of the firm opinion that there is more waste because of the complexity and inefficiency of distribution than in any other economic phase of our existence.

Let us reduce distribution to a few concrete cases, easily understood and see if we can't offer a few suggestions.

A manufacturer of ladies' coats in New York City sells a number of his coats to Jones, Smith or Brown in Boston. He sells these coats at $21.50 each. This cost represents the actual value of the cotton, buttons, designing, sewing on the machines, trimmings, linings, labor on all these essentials in their natural and finished states and a profit for everybody as the coats come through the varied processes.

Delivered into my house from the store, for somebody to wear, there will be nothing more of value added to one of these coats. Even the name of the store has been sewed into the neck-band by the manufacturer. But when that $21.50 coat reaches my house, the price to me is $42.50 or more, generally an advance of over 100 per cent above the entire cost of receiving the coat onto the floor at Jones', Smith's or Brown's.

The operator in the factory, asking for a raise of 25 cents a coat for sewing it, the advance of 2 cents on the transportation of the coat from New York to Boston on the part of the New Haven or the Boston & Albany road are worthy of front-page news stories, but they don't effect the price of the coat one per cent.

You have heard a great deal about the United Shoe Machinery Company as a Trust that fed on the heart's blood of the public. Buy a pair of $15 shoes at any retail store in Boston and you are paying into the United Shoe Machinery about 20 cents to 25 cents royalty. The entire cost of manufacturing is around $7. The rest goes to the retailer.

Read some morning in the papers that beef has been jumped $1.00 a hundred pounds in Chicago by the beef-trust always "the trust," although the real name is Swift & Co., Cudahy or Armour. The cost of the beef should thus be 1 cent more per pound to the butcher, when his present stock is exhausted. But does he wait until his present stock is gone before he advances his price? He does not.   He does it as soon as he hears the news.

Does he advance his prices 1 cent a pound, as the packers have done?   He does not.   He jumps the price several cents and utters terrible things about the heartlessness of "the trust," while inwardly reckoning up the extra profit on your order.

When the restaurant or hotel-man gets the news, he is at a disadvantage, but only temporarily, nothing keeps him at a disadvantage very long. If it is general news that meat has been advanced in Chicago, it will be all right to jump the prices on the menu.   It would be an insult to his patrons to add 1 cent to an order for steak or beef, although that is the added cost per pound to him and he doesn't serve a pound in an order.   So he adds 10 cents to the order or 1000 per cent more than the Chicago packers have added.

But nobody complains of the restaurant man or the hotel proprietor.   The day of the advance in prices at the hotel two intelligent business men sit down to dinner.   "What's this?" asks No. 1, "An order of beef gone up from 75 cents to 85 cents?"

"Sure," remarks No. 2, "I read in the morning paper that beef is up a dollar in Chicago."

"The robbers!" answers No. 1, reconciled.   "I wish the Federal Government would get at the bottom of this Beef Trust. They'll ruin us if we don't look out."

Please don't understand me as holding blameless the clothing manufacturer, the railroad, the Shoe Machinery Syndicate or the beef packers, but they are no more responsible for the high retail prices of merchandise than I am. I don't know but that a careful analysis of these few sources that I cite might show that they have reduced the wholesale costs of manufactured products. The point is quite clearly shown that the shifting prices at wholesale are not honestly reflected at retail.

If the National Biscuit Company reduces its prices 5 percent, the retail price of Uneeda Crackers stays at 8 cents. But if the Boston & Maine railroad jumps the transportation charge 2 cents a can for a 10-quart can of milk, the price of milk automatically goes up 1 cent a quart all over Boston.

If the retailers made a net profit that these illustrations indicate, they would all be millionaires in short order. But the fact is that most of these excessive charges are wasted.

Excessive rents, excessive clerk hire, necessitated by rush hours in stores and markets, a low volume of business per day, when averaged over the entire year, puts a tax of 100 per cent for distribution upon all goods consumed by the public, whether automobiles, furniture, groceries, clothing, milk or medicine.

We have not yet reduced retailing to a science. It is in a crude state. It is more heartless than the most cold-blooded trust. It will not be attacked by the newspapers because they are kept alive by the retailers' advertising. Without retailers' advertising, no big newspaper could live a year. So they point the finger of scorn at the Beef Trust and the Biscuit Trust for advancing prices 5 eer cent, while the big retail advertisers are taking more from the public than all the others put together, and they put absolutely no value into the goods. All they do is distribute them.

We must learn how to retail our merchandise. The U. S. parcel-post has helped out considerably. But the field of retail distribution is a hard one to center public attention upon, as the great public medium, the newspapers, are tied hands and feet.

We must explain to the big retailers themselves, the need of concentrated effort along better lines and when the newspapers find out that their advertisers are willing to have the entire intelligence of the public centered on the problem of Distribution, then we will get somewhere. Otherwise it is to be a slow process.

ON FAKE ADVERTISING

ON FAKE ADVERTISING

FOR years various organizations have tried to stop advertising that misrepresented the value of the article advertised. These organizations were voluntary organizations and in nearly every instance they produced excellent results. At least they threw a moral scare into the fake advertiser.

The strange thing about it is that it was necessary for any body of men to organize to bring about the cessation of fake advertisers. The burden should have been upon the duly chosen officers of the law. But these functioned not. Like the lilies of the fields they toiled not.

I firmly believe that if somebody offered to sell $10 shoes for $2 that the district Attorney's office in any county would pay no attention to the advertisement. It would remain for some other shoe dealer, in self protection to start proceedings or to see that they were started by somebody. What's the answer?

The answer lies in the fact that criminal prosecutions are like all other things—they are governed by self interest. Little old self preservation or selfishness is the dominating factor in nearly everything.

You will say that there have been many cases where fake advertisers have been exposed by officials. This is true, but in nine cases out of ten you will find that if the official on the job took voluntary cognizance of the fake and proceeded against the faker then the publicity was particularly desirable at that time.

Fake advertising of merchandise is more easily detected by the public than fake advertising of a financial nature. The latter is hard to detect for the very reason that the most convincing advertisements get the best results and the faker is not limited to the truth. His object is to sell stocks and sell them quick. So he puts into his advertising statements all those things that will tend to make the advertisement sound truthful.

That is why so much fake financial advertising comes and goes without prosecution. By the time the proposition is investigated and found to be a fraud the damage has been done and the promotor has gone to some other field of operation.

Local advertisers have made the fake advertiser of merchandise practically a thing of the past. The fake financial advertiser is still a menace. He can be eliminated in one way. We offer the remedy.

Enact a Federal Law, using the post office department as the reason for making it National in scope, compelling every advertiser of a financial offering of stocks or bonds of all kinds to file with the United States Treasurer a sworn statement of the actual physical value of the property or business enterprise behind the stock or bond, this report to be filed before any offering can be made to the public. Further, make it a criminal offence for failure to file or for filing false information and a greater offence to sell shares except upon the actual information in the report.

Somehow or other promoters are more in fear of the Federal government than they are of the local government. If the plan here suggested is put into operation, the sale of stock and bonds will be facilitated and the advertiser of fake stocks and bonds will go out of business in the open. Swindling under cover will go on as before but the saving to the people will run into the tens of millions of dollars annually.

ON OUIJA BOARDS

ON OUIJA BOARDS

SOME people don't believe in Ouija Boards. But then, there are many people, even in this enlightened age, who don't believe in Santa Claus. Whether you are a believer in Ouija Boards or not you must admit the subject offers possibilities for discussion and we will now proceed to disgust it.

The Ouija Board as an indoor sport is not new. The present fervor is merely a revival. It had a preliminary run several years ago but didn't seem to get over as strongly as it has in its recent recurrence. It is no longer a toy. It has reached the dignity of a cult. It numbers among its devotees many who are regarded as people of more than average attainments.

The idea of the Ouija Board as an accelerator of spiritual contact is a good idea. It is so good that it has been copyrighted and is protected by the United States Government. Having just passed an Amendment doing away with distilled spirits for beverage purposes it seems only fair that a paternal government should take on the protection of other spirits that can at will, be drawn from the wood of the Ouija Board.

The true Ouijarian is a believer. He believes because he has faith. He is able and inordinately willing to furnish evidence in proof of his contention regarding the efficacy of the Ouija Board. Hear ye! Hear ye!

A friend of mine who Ouija-izes with unflagging zeal at every opportunity proffers the following instance.

One night she was holding her faithful little Ouija on her knees. Her finger tips were touching the tabloid table that tops the board. She asked the Board the direct question, "How old is my father?" Without a moment's hesitation the prow of the planchette began to spin around the Board and spell out the answer. An excited bystander wrote out the answer as follow, "I AM VERY HAPPY." Explaining the answer my friend assured me that her father was dead and that this showed that his spirit couldn't be fooled but that it wanted her to know that he was happy.

Another Ouija follower gave me an equally concrete example of Ouijaism. He had the lights all out except one. This one had a pink shade over it. He never felt more in tune with the board than on this occasion. Let him tell it—full quotes.

"I felt a mystic influence about me. I was alone except for Ouija. I asked a question out loud. I felt that the answer would come, I believed. I said 'Ouija tell me if my love is reciprocated?' I waited for the answer. Little beads of perspiration stood out on my forehead. No answer came. I repeated the question whispering it, this time, and then waited. Slowly the planchette began to move over the smooth surface of the board. I thought of those immortal words of Omar, 'The moving finger writes.' I watched the little table. Patiently it began to spell out its message. The letters 'C-H-A-S-S' came out distinctly and then the planchette refused to function further.

"I knew there was an answer to be found in these letters. I puzzled my brain for hours. Then like a flash, it came to me. The Ouija Board on this occasion was controlled by the spirit of an old friend who had passed into spirit land four years ago. He was a Dutch Comedian and always joked with me in quaint dialect. He wouldn't say 'Yes'. He would speak to me in the same old intimate way as of yore. He would say 'Chass' instead of 'Yes'.

"You can't imagine the joy that came to me with this discovery. Often I had doubted my Ouija Board. But with absolute, scientific, convincing evidence before me of its marvelous, yes, its supernatural powers, how could I remain anything but a firm believer in the future?"

He closed his eyes and his recital at the same time. I was so overcome that I turned my head away. It was nothing short of uncanny. So simple, so eloquent, so concise, so reasonable. And yet—

As we—to return to the editorial department for the nonce or the noncence if you prefer the accusative case—stated in the opening round of this bout, there are still those who don't believe in Ouija Boards. How such unbelief can flaunt itself in the face of such evidence as we have here so carefully connoted is something that we cannot understand unless it be on the old Lincolnian maxim that a Board in the lap is worth two boards in the fence. You can't understand a Ouija Board unless you have wood in your head. In other words it is a knotty problem no matter how you view it.

ON GOING TO CHURCH

ON GOING TO CHURCH

THE fact that ten times as many people attend the movies as go to church isn't a fact. It is a lie. What the man who started this mis-statement on its travels probably meant to say was that the total admissions of all the movie houses in a year would be ten times the number of those who attend all the church services during a year. For the sake of conservatism let us include as church services the Billy Sunday revivals wherever he may be tabernackling.

But that there are ten times as many people who attend movies as attend churches is, of course, ridiculous. Some regular church goers, once-a-month or so, are frequenters of movies every other day. They go to the movies because they like them. They go to church as a sort of a duty. Let's see if we can't straighten it out.

Should a man or woman or a child go to church unless there is some pleasure in it? Many will say "yes" and adduce the idea that going to church is a sacred obligation, that this is the only way to keep in touch with the heavenly father etc. etc. Why keeping in touch with the infinite should be so dull and uninteresting that people shrink from it is something yet to be explained. We can't accept the premise as correct.

Years ago, when a man went out and got drunk, instead of going to church, the deacons or the ministers used to say that the devil had lured him away. But the churches are not competing with the saloons any more. The saloons are gone forever.

The movies are not conducted as competitors of the churches. No movie house runs a line on the screen telling people not to go to church. On the contrary every film, if it teaches a lesson at all, teaches the evils of immorality and advises people to be good. While propaganda is not the main offering of the movie houses there is a sprinkling of it in nearly every feature picture. Not a picture that has ever been screened in America ever hinted that drunkenness was desirable, that robbery was justifiable or that murder could be committed with impunity. More effectively than any minister could hope to tell the story has the honest young lover always won the girl in the story as told at the movie house. People don't go to movies to avoid being moralized at. They love it. But—

They like it doped up in pleasant dress. They like it in sugar coated pill form. They like it with a little rag-time. They don't like it in dull monotone. They don't like it the way their grandfather used to be compelled to take it when he was a little boy. They want it as of the year 1921, which is three hundred and one years after the Pilgrims laid the corner stone of an American democracy and founded the famous line of Plymouth Rock hens, who lay the foundation of our breakfast table menu.

People go to the movies because the movies are up to date. If a movie manager's business falls off he changes his program. He doesn't pray to God for a revival of big audiences. He sends a hurry up call to Jesse Lasky or Goldwyn or D. W. Griffith and says "Give me a line of pictures that the people want to see." And he gets them.

But the church with a seating capacity of 600 will drag along with a Sunday morning audience of 100, patiently waiting for Easter and the Sunday before Christmas or a visit from the Bishop to give it a boost for one day and never do a thing to look into the cause for the poor attendance. The church people can put the blame onto God if they wish to but if he is to be blamed for keeping people from going to church then he should be given credit for sending them to the movies in droves. Surely if he didn't want them at the movies he wouldn't let them go. You see where such a method of reasoning would lead us. God has no direct bearing on the question. It is a little problem that we can settle for ourselves, with the brains that God gave us to settle little problems.

The reason that people go to movies frequently and to church only occasionally is because they like the movies better. A good movie is a treat. A poor sermon is a disgrace. Most churches are poorly conducted, the services are dull, there isn't any pep to the music and the sermons are in keeping with the rest of the show.

What the churches need is jazz. Wake up the audiences! Retire the out-worn ministers. Give better salaries for better preachers! Hire the best available singers! Advertise the attractions! Put on a better show than the movies and the churches will get bigger crowds. People are entitled to an entertainment even when they are being good. They get it at the movies. Until they get it at church they will go to the movies in preference. You can't get around it by prayer. Action is the only solution.

ON THE ULTIMATE PHOTO-PLAYS

ON THE ULTIMATE PHOTO-PLAYS

THERE have been so many "expert" opinions ventured during the past year that a mere observer of picture-plays must needs move cautiously in expressing himself on the subject of "what the Public wants."

As a student of entertainment and a some-time writer of stories, I offer the following analytical comment on the trend of the movies, not merely as something that I am hopeful will be, but something that I really believe must be the ultimate picture—I mean the dominant, majority-picture of the near future.

One thing is established beyond all doubt. The motion-picture patrons of today know good photography, recognize good acting, laugh at fakes, yawn at dullness and are not thrilled simply because the press agents of the Distributing Agency predict that they will be. After five years of constantly improving pictures the public of nowadays are a pretty wise crowd, and the producers who don't cut their positive prints accordingly will find it out, maybe, when it is too late.

A while ago the stage was going through the throes of dramatization of novels, parts of the bible, famous and infamous trials, short stories and well-known advertisements. A prominent dramatist called up a big play-producer, one day, and said "Dave, I've got one of the most brilliant ideas that has struck a New York playright this year. We have dramatized about everything except the New York Public Library, but guess what I am going to dramatize?"

"Give it up," said Dave.

"I have decided," said the playright, and his voice shook with supressed emotion, "I have decided to dramatize a play."

"Good heavens!" shouted the big producer "you don't mean it. The most original thing I've heard in years. I guarantee, without seeing it, to produce it."

I feel that it is about time that the motion picture field gets ready to secure its own writers, picturize its own stories, and photograph some photo-plays. Some producers are already feeling their way around the dark rooms. Very soon we shall see screen productions of stories written especially for the screen by men who think in pictures because they have trained themselves so to think.

I have written a few novels, a lot of verse, a modicum of sketches, a play or two, an endless raft of short stories, articles, essays and advertisements without end. Recently, some well-paid-for acceptances of scenarios have put me into the motion picture field.

I have found that the style of presentation is so entirely different, the original conception of story, of climax, of holding the interest is so disassociated from all other kinds of writing that I am quite convinced the writing of picture-plays is in a class by itself.

Augustus Thomas sits at his desk and thinks up four situations called acts, into which he puts all his characters and tells his story.

C. Gardner Sullivan or any of the better photoplay dramatists sit at their typewriters and for every one of Mr. Thomas' acts their minds create forty or fifty scenes, interspersed with close-ups, sub-titles and flashes. Instead of conversations they think up scenes that indicate what the conversation would naturally be in the situation shown. Only in cases of any possible doubt do they supply the conversation with sub-titles and quotation marks.

Many a short story and many a long story find a market because of the cleverness of the author in the use of the written word. But to write scenarios in the hope that clever sub-titles will put the pictures across is a wild dream.

Quite a few productions fell dismally back onto the shelves because the producers fooled themselves into thinking that a popular story in magazine form necessarily meant a popular photo-play. Skinner's Dress Suit fitted the classic form of Bryant Washburn in a most wonderful way. But it had a dandy story to go with it. The short story could have followed the screen version just as well as the screen play followed the short story. If you don't believe me, just watch the crop of bloomers that will scenario themselves out of the Saturday Evening Post within the next year or two.

I heard from a producer the other day, and was informed that the firm had decided hereafter to screen only novels that had attained wide popularity. In view of the decision of a big Western publishing house—just made—not to produce any more novels except those taken from big screen successes, I am wondering what would happen to any poor author who got between these two firms and waited—one refusing to screen his story until it was published as a novel and the other refusing to consider his manuscript as a novel until it had been released all over the country as a successful photo-play. The only course open to him would be to write a story called "Starvation" and leave the manuscript to the Art Museum.

The best plays ever seen were written by play-rights for production on the stage. The best photo-plays will be written by photo-dramatists who write in scenes, think in picture-climaxes and visualize their thoughts in motion-photo-grapy.

As to the cleanliness of the subjects, the decency of the photo-play field and its ultimate moral tone, these things always work themselves out automatically. The names that live in drama are all clean names. A man who can't play the Keith Circuit because his act is unfitted for nice audiences will soon find himself without steady work on any circuit. The burlesque houses of today would not produce the burlesque shows of twenty years ago.

George M. Cohan never wrote an unclean joke, never put over a questionable line in all the shows or sketches he has written. Only a very careless man would suggest that Cohan is not fairly successful as a purveyor of entertainment.

The ultimate motion-picture plays will be highly specialized, well-acted, clearly photographed dramas of movement, subtitled as little as possible, with logical climaxes, well-spaced thrills, clean comedy of situation, consistent plots and satisfactory endings.

Such plays can only be produced by experienced directors, working with equally experienced actors, scene builders, camera-men, getting their inspiration from manuscripts written for the purpose by men and women who think of stories only in terms of photography and whose stage vision is as wide as the wide, wide world.

ON INTERRUPTIONS

ON INTERRUPTIONS

ONE phase of mentality, or lack of it, that has often been forced upon my attention is the weakness that some people have for interrupting. Butting in might be a better term, but, of course, it would never do to use such a clearly-comprehended expression in what purports to be an essay. So we will—after this interruption—get back to a given point and start again.

Interruptions are not confined to any special stratum of society. From meetings of the vestrymen of the church, up to, and including barber shops, the weakness is manifested.

I recall one barber shop to which I am forced to go occasionally for a hair-cut. I have noted that, regardless of how dull may be the shop when I enter it, no sooner am I seated in the chair of the head-barber—by "head" I mean "chief" or "first"—than every barber in the shop discovers that he has something of the utmost importance to say to the man who is supposed to be giving his attention to me. Not another customer in the shop. Not a word had been said or a thing done for the half hour up to the time when I interrupted the peace and quiet of their place of business.

And yet—

My entrance seems to have been a signal for all kinds of activity and all of it must, of necessity, be predicated upon the spoken word and this spoken word is an interchange of language between the man working on my hair and his numerous assistants—know in the composite as "the help." That, I shall not attempt to explain.

"When is the towel man coming?" "Will I hone Mr. Seeley's razor?" "Did you notice how cold it was this morning at 5 o'clock?" "Will I go out and get that bay rum now, or wait till later?" and one million other questions are hurled at the occupied chair of otherwise empty barber shops all over the United States, every day. Whether this is part of the course in Italy, the alma mater of our tonsorial system, is something with which I am not familiar.

That it holds good in all the boot-blacking parlors, every man who ever has his shoes shined will bear me witness. Go into any of Professor Joe's places, anywhere in America. Let every chair be empty. Let the entire force be sound asleep dreaming of Dante or D'Annunzio or The Acropolis, if it is that kind of a shop, and get into a chair, thus indicating that you wish your shoes cleaned.

Long before the instructor—full professorships are conferred only upon the owners—has reached that point in his work where you feel it necessary to caution him about your sox not needing any paste, every other man in the place is on his feet and asking questions of the one who from time to time pays a little attention to your shoes.

Does he ignore his countrymen and chide them? Does he speak to them sharply and call their attention to the fact that he is busy with a customer? Forsooth, he does not. In fact, he seems to take an uncanny interest in everything they say.

With a box of red paste in one hand—I'm assuming you wear black shoes—and with the other hand in close proximity to the knee of your light trousers or leaning gracefully upon it, he acts as the switchboard of a bunch of overseas jargon that would make the press gallery at the Olympic games think they had been cut off from the world.

Of course, interruptions are not confined to the higher forms of industry. You get them even in banking circles or in Doctor's offices or at the Somerset Club. No place is immune.

You wait two hours in order to have a strictly private interview with some man in an office which proclaims in gilt letters to everybody that it is "private". Do you get a private interview? You do not.

In the midst of your best sentence—something corresponding in your speech to the second paragraph of Lincoln's address at Gettysburg—you are stopped short by a ring of the phone and you learn, with much pleasure, that Mr. So-and-So's limousine is to be laid up for one more day and he will have to get along as best he can with the little old last year's landaulet.   He takes five minutes to tell you about the rotten service he's getting at the garage and you sit like a dummy afraid to interrupt him and put the interview back onto the main line where it ought to be.

I imagine you get me, together with the moral of these few observations, so, without further interruptions, the next subject will be in order.

ON WHY NOT WORRY?

ON WHY NOT WORRY?

THE idea seems to be quite prevalent that mental activity is conductive to ill-health whereas the contrary is the truth. Health comes from an active mind, a mind that is working at concert pitch, sending directions to the heart, and telling that engine to keep busy in the circulation department.

A wrong conception of mental activity has crept into the minds of many people. For lack of the ability to diagnose many cases, innumerable physicians have spread the false propaganda that worry brings about ill-health, that worry is a curse that must be eradicated or else the ill-health will continue and after elaborating on the proposition they look their patients full in the face and with profound sombreness say "You are worrying too much. That's what is the matter. You must stop worrying and you will be all right."

Of all the stupid things ever advanced by the medical profession—and they have surely put out a full quota of stupidity—this is the essence. To intelligent people it is a joke. But to those who still believe that a Doctor's diploma carries with it some magical power, it is a menace. This little paper on the subject will not stop it, but if it saves

135

only one trusting man or woman from a life of misery or sets some doctor straight it will be doing something.

Let us go at it, logically, and with a concrete example in mind.

A woman feels ill. Her stomach is not doing its work or she has a back-ache or she has frequent head-aches. She, naturally, consults her doctor. He prescribes the usual stuff. She takes it. It doesn't work. The aches or the disorders continue. He looks wise—at least, he tries to do so. He shakes his head. He becomes deep. Then he pulls the same old dope. Doctors always do the same thing, that is, unless they are "specialists". Then they charge more for doing it.

"Have you been worrying, of late?" he asks his patient. Has she been worrying? Why, the poor simp, can't he tell, without asking a single question, that she has been worrying about the rent, and the wash-lady, and the new girl and the income tax and her husband's spats and Mildred's new dresses and the gown she is to wear at the Alpha Alpha Club reception and 4279 other things that engage the attention of every intelligent woman who isn't dead from her heels up? Her brain is active, keyed up, she is responsive to heat and cold, she takes an interest in her family and in the life of the neighborhood. Worry? Sure she worries, if the correct definition for worry is the one that the Doctors would make us swallow as though it were a dose of quinine.

So the poor woman has to say "Yes", in a frightened voice and the Doctor smiles and says, "I thought so. You are neurasthenic. You must stop worrying or you will be a nervous wreck!"

Get the picture. A sick woman, a big husky Doctor getting paid for telling her to stop worrying and intimating that every time she uses her brain she is endangering her health. And he expects her to stop thinking just because he says so.

Does she go home and do what the nice, kind Doctor man tells her? She does not. She tries to think less of her regular duties and the harder she tries the more she thinks. Then comes the terrible thought that she is "worrying", that she is not following the Doctor's instructions. Naturally, she becomes irritated more and more.

She begins to feel pains that she never knew existed. She begins to experience mental anguish that she never knew before. And she goes to the Doctor again and explains it all to him. Waste of effort. Instead of convincing him, as it should, that he is making a mental wreck out of his patient with his dam fool talk, he accepts her story as a confirmation of his analysis. So he tells her again, not to worry, that it will ruin her nervous system and she goes home and tries to do the impossible. She tries not to think. She might just as well try not to breathe, permanently. At least she can stop breathing for short spells, but the brain never stops working and for a Doctor to tell a woman "not to worry" is to tell her "not to think". It can't be done.

He is false in his premise. Years ago the same profession used to bleed people. They now shoot blood into them. They used to keep the windows of a sick room closed. Now they open every window they can find and give folks oxygen from a tank. They used to laugh at Dentists. Now, every Doctor has his pet dentist to whom he sends his patients. They ought to go to the dentist first. Then they might not need the Doctor. Why multiply examples? Everybody knows that most Doctor's books are out-of-date before the books get to the bindery. Why they waste the fees for having them copyrighted is something I can't understand.

And their latest fetish is "worry". Being something ascribed to the brain, and therefore hidden, they can go as far as they like. If they analyzed the trouble as gall stones or appendicitis or something that the Mayo brothers could show, in thirty seconds, was or wasn't so, they wouldn't get away with it at all. But "worry"? Why, they read into it every brain function, and hypnotize the patient to such an extent that every time she uses her brain she feels that she is weakening her system and, of course, such mental activity can have but one result—the worst.

The solution of this problem is simple. I call upon every "Doctor", every "neurologist", every "psychologist", or what not to tell their patients to do all the worrying they please. Tell them that the word "worry" has crept into the medical language under false pretenses. Tell them the truth, that mental activity only becomes "worry" when some Doctor tells his patient that it is effecting his health and, of course, the health, from that time on, is in danger.

Let a Doctor tell a man that "walking" is bad for him and the man will be red in the face at the end of a hundred yard walk. Tell the same man that walking is the best thing he can do and he will walk two miles without puffing, even though his heart is organically weak.

It all comes from the mind. Tell a man that his mental activity is endangering his health and of course his health becomes involved just because it is in his mind all the time thereafter.

Tell every man or woman that they can do all the worrying they feel like, that it is the best thing they can do, that it is mental activity that stimulates the action of the heart and improves the circulation and they will read into every mental activity some good that is to result in their general health.

Most people can't rise above the opinion of Doctors. That is why they consult them. Let's have done with this "worry" bunk. It is a danger to the community. It is founded on a false hypothesis. You can't make a man feel well by telling him that every normal activity is making him ill. Therefore tell him that his activity is conducive to health and see how quick he will respond.

It is logic. It is psychology. Why not worry?